COUNTRIES IN OUR WORLD

AUSTRALIA
IN OUR WORLD

Aleta Moriarty

A+

Smart Apple Media

Published by Smart Apple Media
P.O. Box 3263, Mankato, Minnesota 56002

Printed in the United States of America at Corporate Graphics, in North Mankato, Minnesota.

Published by arrangement with the Watts Publishing Group Ltd., London.

Library of Congress Cataloging-in-Publication Data

Moriarty, Aleta.
   Australia in our world / by Aleta Moriarty.
      p. cm. -- (Countries in our world)
   Summary: "Describes the economy, government, and culture of Australia today and discusses Australia's influence of and relations with the rest of the world"--Provided by publisher.
   Includes bibliographical references and index.
   ISBN 978-1-59920-385-0 (library binding)
   1. Australia--Juvenile literature. I. Title.
   DU96.M665 2011
   994.07'2--dc22

                                                                    2009052420

Produced by White-Thomson Publishing Ltd.

Series consultant: Rob Bowden
Editor: Sonya Newland
Designer: Clare Nicholas
Picture researcher: Amy Sparks

Picture Credits
Corbis: Cover (R. Wallace/Stock Photos/zefa), 5 (Richard Eastwood), 12 (Pascal Deloche/Godong), 13 (Dave G. Houser), 14 (John Van Hasselt), 21 (Tim Wimborne/Reuters), 25 (Pool/Reuters), 26 (Andrew Taylor/Pool/Reuters), 28 (Franz-Marc Frei); **Dreamstime:** 9 (Ashley Whitworth), 19 (Cameo), 20 (Matthew Weinel); **Fotolia:** 15 (Jobhopper); **iStock:** 10 (Cat London), 27 (Scott Hailstone); **Photoshot:** 18 (World Pictures), 22 (Blend Images); **Shutterstock:** 6 (G. Tipene), 7 (I. Birznieks), 8 (Debra James), 11 (Andrea B), 16 (Styve Reineck), 23 (gmwnz), 24 (Phillip Minnis), 29 (Nicole Paton); **WTPix:** 1, 17.

1207
32010

9 8 7 6 5 4 3 2 1

Contents

Introducing Australia

Australia is the sixth largest country in the world, and the only nation to occupy an entire continent. Aboriginal or indigenous Australians are among the oldest peoples on Earth, but it was only quite recently that people from other parts of the world began to settle in Australia.

Land Down Under

The name Australia means "southern land." Australia is located in the southern hemisphere, which is why it is sometimes called "Down Under" by people who live in the northern hemisphere. It is located between the Pacific and the Indian oceans, south of Asia. Its nearest neighbor is Papua New Guinea, which lies to the northeast. New Zealand and Indonesia are also close by. Australia has many different landscapes—from snowy mountains and tropical beaches, to sprawling dry deserts and lush rain forests.

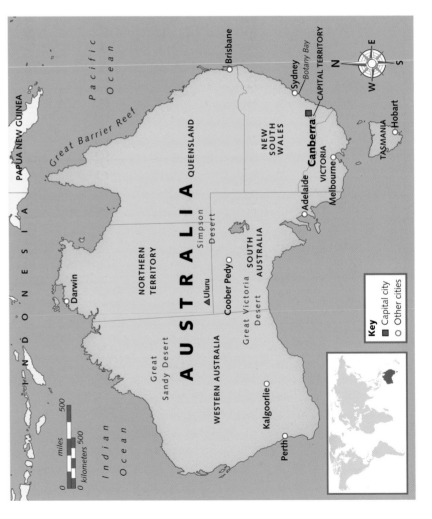

▶ *Australia is the world's largest inhabited island and the smallest continent. It is divided into six states and two territories.*

Large Country, Small Population

Australia's land mass is about the same size as the 48 mainland states of the United States, minus Alaska. Despite this, it has one of the lowest population densities in the world— only 6.8 people per square mile (2.6 people per sq km). Only Mongolia and Namibia have lower population densities than Australia.

▼ *The population of Australia is concentrated in coastal cities like Hobart, on the island of Tasmania. Here people gather at a busy marketplace.*

IT'S A FACT!

There are more species of marsupials in Australia than any other mammal — around 260 different types, including the wombat, koala, and kangaroo. Marsupials give birth to unformed offspring that then develop further in the female's pouch.

Settlers from Overseas

Australia's Aboriginal or Indigenous (native) population has lived in the country for more than 50,000 years. For most of that time, they were cut off from the rest of the world, undisturbed by other settlers. In 1770, however, the English explorer Captain James Cook sailed to Australia and claimed the east coast as a colony of Britain. The first Europeans settled in Australia in January 1788, when the First Fleet sailed into Botany Bay under the command of Captain Arthur Phillip. Since then, more and more immigrants have moved to Australia from all over the world.

A Multicultural Society

Today, Australia is one of the most multicultural places on Earth, with people of all different nationalities. There is a strong "East-meets-West" feel, because while many people from Europe now live there, it is very close to the Asia-Pacific region and attracts settlers from there, too. Australia's patchwork of cultures is bound together by a love of international cuisine, outdoor activities, and sports.

▶ *A statue of English Captain James Cook stands in Hyde Park, Sydney, commemorating the arrival of the first European people in Australia.*

BASIC DATA	
Official name: **Commonwealth of Australia**	
Capital: **Canberra**	
Size: **2,967,909 sq miles (7,686,850 sq km)**	
Population: **21,262,641 (2009 est.)**	
Currency: **Australian dollar**	

Australia in the World

Because of its history as a British colony, Australia has traditionally had very strong links with the UK, as well as with the U.S. and European countries. It also enjoys good relations with Asian countries because of its close geographic location, particularly Japan and China, who are very important trading partners with Australia. Since the 1990s, Australia's economy has been one of the fastest growing in the world, and the country is becoming increasingly influential in world trade. However, like many other countries, Australia suffered from the global financial crisis that began in 2008, and there was a downturn in trade.

▼ *These Chinese Australians have just taken part in a parade in Sydney to celebrate the Chinese New Year.*

Landscapes and Environment

Australia is a hot, dry country, with a tropical climate in the north and a temperate climate in the south and east.

It has many different landscapes, from mountains to deserts. Australia is particularly famous for its long, sandy coastline and its huge, dry interior known as the Outback.

A Desert Country

Australia is one of the flattest, driest continents on Earth. It has the lowest rainfall of any of the world's inhabited continents—70 percent of Australia gets less than 20 inches (500 mm) of rainfall each year. Three-quarters of Australia is desert—an area about the same size as Mongolia. Because it is so dry in the center of the country, most Australians live along the coast. Australia is home to three of the world's top 20 largest deserts—the Great Victoria Desert, Simpson Desert, and Great Sandy Desert.

THE HOME OF...

Uluru

Uluru is a large rock formation in central Australia. It is a famous landmark and is considered sacred by Indigenous Australians. The Aboriginal landowners have asked visitors not to climb the rock because of this, but some tourists still hike up Uluru. Some of them have stolen pieces of rock from the site, but thousands of pieces have been sent back to central Australia from all over the world, because people think the pieces have caused them bad luck.

▶ *The sacred Aboriginal site Uluru stands 2,831 feet (863 m) high, and is a popular tourist destination.*

A Watery World

Australia has more beaches than any other country in the world—more than 18,641 miles (30,000 km) of coastline. Off the northeastern coast lies the Great Barrier Reef, the largest coral reef in the world. This stretches over 1,429 miles (2,300 km), and is so large that it can be seen from space. The Great Barrier Reef is under threat from climate change and pollution, but today it is protected as part of the Great Barrier Reef Marine Park, which tries to preserve this unique environment.

▶ *The Great Barrier Reef has long been a popular destination for scuba divers. Care is now being taken to ensure that such activity does not damage the coral.*

PLACE IN THE WORLD

Total area: **2,967,909 sq miles (7,686,850 sq km)**

Percentage of world land area: **5.2%**

World ranking: **6th**

A Unique Habitat

Because Australia is so isolated, it is a unique area of biodiversity. The country is home to between 600,000 and 700,000 plant and animal species, and most of these are unique to Australia. Around 84 percent of Australia's plants, 83 percent of its mammals, and 45 percent of its birds can only be found there.

Bird Migration

Hundreds of migratory water birds, such as plovers, sandpipers, curlews, and snipes, visit Australia every year. Amazingly, these birds make round-trip migrations of up to 16,155 miles (26,000 km) each year between their breeding grounds in the northern hemisphere and their non-breeding areas in the south. These trips are made in several weeks, with brief stops at countries along the way to rest and refuel for the next leg of their journey.

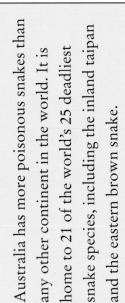

IT'S A FACT!

Australia has more poisonous snakes than any other continent in the world. It is home to 21 of the world's 25 deadliest snake species, including the inland taipan and the eastern brown snake.

▶ The pink cockatoos known as galahs are indigenous to Australia and can be seen all over the country except in the driest parts of the deserts.

Wild Creatures

Early settlers introduced a number of animals such as cats, rabbits, horses, camels, and foxes into Australia. Many of these species have gone feral (wild) and are now threatening Australia's fragile ecosystem. Native wildlife includes kangaroos, koalas, and wombats, as well as deadly creatures such as snakes and spiders.

▼ *Road signs all over Australia warn drivers that there might be kangaroos in the road.*

11

THE HOME OF...

Kangaroo Kingdom

There are 55 different species of kangaroos and wallabies native to Australia. They vary greatly in size and weight, ranging from 1.1 to 198 lbs. (0.5 to 90 kg). Some kangaroos are as tall as humans, and others are as small as domestic cats. Kangaroo babies are called joeys and live in their mother's pouch. Australia's kangaroo population is between 30 and 60 million.

Population and Migration

Australia has a long history of migration. The first Australian residents came to the country between 58,000 and 100,000 years ago, possibly across a land bridge that existed at the time. Since then, 600 to 700 different groups have populated Australia, speaking more than 200 languages.

Penal Colony

During the 1780s, the British decided to transport prisoners to Australia because its own prisons were overflowing. In 1788, the first ships arrived from England, bringing 778 convicts. Most of the prisoners were men under the age of 30, who were being punished for stealing. Once they got to Australia, the convicts were put to work making roads, chopping down trees, and building bridges and barracks.

▶ *Australia is one of the most multicultural nations in the world. Here, young people of different ethnic backgrounds come together to celebrate World Youth Day.*

Gold Bonanza

As gold fever struck the world during the 1850s, migrants moved to Australia from Ireland, Britain, and China to search for riches in Australia's goldfields. At this time, many people lived in makeshift tents and houses in big groups around the goldfields. The Immigration Restriction Act was put in place in 1901. This was nicknamed the "White Australia Policy" because it stopped non-Europeans from immigrating to Australia. The Act was overturned in 1966 to allow skilled non-Europeans to enter Australia.

Changing Australia

After World War II (1939–45), the Australian government believed that if it did not populate the country, it would not be able to defend itself in the future. Many immigrants, fleeing from the devastating effects of the war, were allowed to come from Europe to Australia. People arrived from countries such as Malta, Italy, Yugoslavia, and Britain. Two million immigrants arrived in Australia between 1947 and 1967.

13

▶ In the nineteenth century, people flocked to Australia in search of gold, and it can still be found there. This boy is panning for gold for fun in Sovereign Hill, Victoria.

GOING GLOBAL

More than 6.5 million migrants have settled in Australia since 1945, and it is now home to people from more than 200 countries. Over 680,000 of these arrived under humanitarian programs, initially as displaced persons and more recently as refugees, most of them from countries in the Middle East, Asia, and Africa.

An Important Contribution

Migrants have made an important contribution to Australian society. For example, the Chinese-born Australian citizen Victor Chang performed Australia's first heart and lung transplant. Eye doctor Fred Hollows was born in New Zealand, but settled in Australia. He restored the sight of thousands of people.

The Indigenous Issue

As more people from overseas have settled in Australia, Indigenous Australians have been marginalized, and today only about two percent of the population is Indigenous. They experience significant disadvantages compared to the rest of the population, including lower life expectancy and high

PLACE IN THE WORLD
Population: **21,262,641 (2009 est.)**
Percentage of world total: **0.32%**
World ranking: **51st**

levels of unemployment. They have lost much of their traditional land and they are often victims of racism. This has attracted widespread international criticism of the Australian government, and human rights groups all over the world have campaigned to improve the lives of Indigenous Australians.

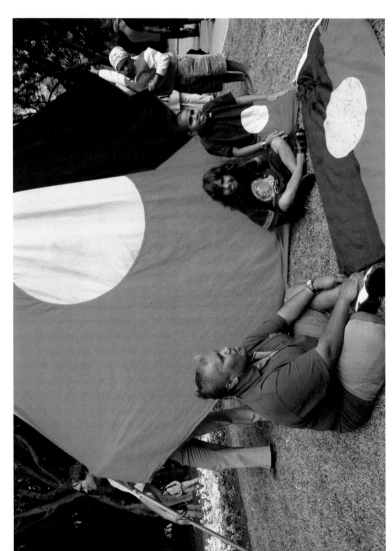

▶ *These Indigenous Australians are protesting against the loss of their traditional lands. In recent years, the government has worked toward improving treatment of Aboriginals.*

14

City Living

Over three-quarters of Australians live in cities. Australian cities offer some of the highest standards of living anywhere in the world; Sydney is frequently ranked among the top 10 cities to live in for its high quality of life. However, a good quality of life doesn't come cheap—Sydney also ranks as the 15th most expensive city in the world.

▼ *Melbourne is the second largest city in Australia, with a population of nearly four million.*

IT'S A FACT!

Australia's population is increasing by one person every 1 minute and 37 seconds. There is a birth every 1 minute and 51 seconds and a death every 3 minutes and 48 seconds. One person migrates to Australia from another country every 2 minutes and 55 seconds.

Culture and Lifestyles

Australia's multicultural population means that its society reflects the influence of cultures and traditions from all over the world. In addition, Aboriginal Australian culture is one of the oldest still surviving, dating back between 40,000 and 65,000 years.

Indigenous Art

Australian Aboriginal art is the oldest surviving artistic tradition in the world. Aboriginal rock paintings can be found all over the country. Paintings found in the Kakadu region, created more than 20,000 years ago, provide one of the longest historical records of any group of people in the world. In some parts of Australia, Indigenous rock art dates back more than 30,000 years, making this artwork seven times older than the pyramids of Egypt, 15 times older than the Great Wall of China, and 60 times older than Michelangelo's Sistine Chapel.

▼ *Indigenous rock paintings often depict characters from the Dreaming—the period when Australian Aboriginals believe the Earth was created. This rock art at Kakadu is the most recent, painted in the 1960s.*

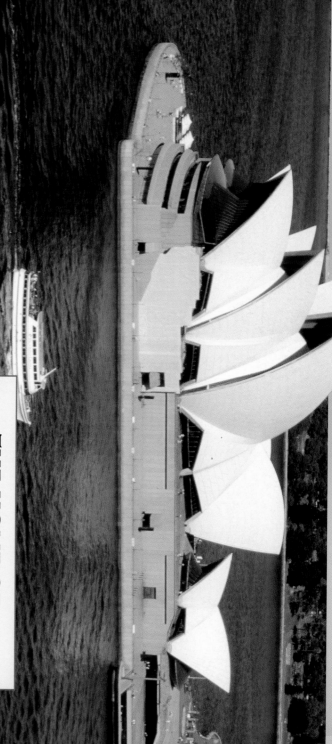

▶ *The Sydney Opera House, in Sydney Harbor, is one of the most famous buildings in the world.*

Food Favorites

Nearly one in four Australians today was born overseas, and Australia's immigrants have brought culinary traditions from around the world. This can be seen in the many different types of restaurants. Most Australian towns have a Chinese restaurant, and Lebanese *tabbouleh*, Greek salads, the British Sunday roast, Thai takeout, and Italian pasta are all popular. Australia's top chefs have a multicultural flair that has led to a worldwide demand, and many have left Australia to work in restaurants in other countries. Although Australia has no national dish, the outdoor barbecue is one of the favorite ways of cooking.

17

THE HOME OF...

Sydney Opera House

When it opened in 1973, the Sydney Opera House instantly became a world-famous landmark because of its unusual design, which looks like the sails of a ship. It took more than 15 years to build, and more than a million tiles were used to cover the roof of the building.

Many Beliefs

Although more than 61 percent of Australians are Christians, the country embraces many different religious beliefs that reflect the origins of its people. Around 1.9 percent of the population is Buddhist, and 1.5 percent is Muslim. Around the country there are Catholic and Anglican churches, Hindu, Sikh, and Buddhist temples, Islamic mosques, and Jewish synagogues.

A Sporting Nation

Sports are a popular pastime in Australia. Because the country has a warm climate, Australians enjoy outdoor sports such as surfing, swimming, jogging, and Australian rules football. Every week, around 11 million Australians partake in a sporting event; Australia has some of the most famous sportsmen and women in the world, especially cricketers and swimmers. It participates in many international sporting events, including the Commonwealth and Olympic Games. Along with Greece, Australia has attended more Summer Olympic Games than any other nation, and has hosted the event twice—in Melbourne in 1956 and in Sydney in 2000.

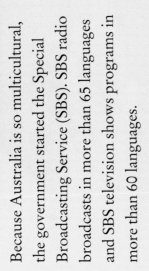

IT'S A FACT!

Because Australia is so multicultural, the government started the Special Broadcasting Service (SBS). SBS radio broadcasts in more than 65 languages and SBS television shows programs in more than 60 languages.

▶ *Children take part in a cricket event at the Adelaide Oval cricket ground.*

Soap Opera Exports

Australian soap operas are popular all around the world. *Home and Away* is a television series that follows the lives of Summer Bay residents. It is broadcast into homes in countries as far away as Canada, Norway, Belgium, the UK, Ireland, and France. Another series, *Neighbors*, is set in the fictional suburb of Erinsborough. It has been shown in the UK, Israel, New Zealand, Belgium, Ireland, Kenya, Barbados, Iceland, and Norway. It is so popular that at times the UK audience has been larger than the total Australian population!

19

Education

In Australia, all children have to go to school until they are 15 or 16, depending on which state they live in. Some children live in settlements in remote areas, too far away from population centers to be able to go to a school. They receive their education in an unusual way—lessons are sent to them by mail, and children work at home. Sometimes they use radios or the Internet and email to communicate with teachers. Australia has one of the highest literacy rates in the world—99 percent of the population can read and write.

▲ *This boy is having lessons at a "school of the air" in Australia's Northern Territory. Children here communicate with teachers via two-way radios.*

FAMOUS AUSTRALIAN

Kylie Minogue (b. 1968)

Australian pop star Kylie Minogue is an international sensation. She has sold more than 60 million albums worldwide and sold out six world tours. Her hit song "Can't Get you out of my Head" reached No. 1 in over 20 countries. She has performed all over the world, including at the closing ceremony of the Sydney Olympics in 2000.

Economy and Trade

Australia is rich in natural resources and highly skilled workers, and it has a long history of farming. This has resulted in a strong, stable economy. Australia's economy is beavily dependent on industries such as farming and mining. Its total exports are around $234.3 billion every year.

▶ *This sign in the town of Coober Pedy shows an opal blower—a machine used to suck rock and dust from the mines.*

Underground Opal World

Most of the world's precious opal gemstones are found in Australia. The world's opal capital is the underground town of Coober Pedy in South Australia. Here, there are even hotels in caves underground. In 1990, the world's largest opal was found here, weighing 11.6 lbs. (5.27 kg)—as much as a big baby!

Gold Galore

Australia is the world's third largest producer of gold. Kalgoorlie, in Western Australia, is the country's richest goldfield. Since they started mining in the "golden mile," miners have found more than 50 million ounces of gold. This is enough to create a gold wire that stretches around the world 315,394 times!

20

Farming

Farmers own and occupy over half of Australia's land. Farming accounts for about three percent of Australia's GDP (gross domestic product), with beef, cotton, sheep, and wheat all farmed in the country. Australian wines are famous worldwide for their rich flavors, and the country exports around 189 million gallons (715 million liters) of wine annually—enough to fill 1,190 Olympic-sized swimming pools! Most Australian farms are family businesses, but this is slowly changing, as farms are getting bigger and more commercial.

▼ *Australia is second only to China in the number of sheep it has. More than 100 million sheep are raised, often on huge ranches.*

GLOBAL LEADER

Coal Mining

Although Australia only ranks fourth in the world in terms of coal reserves (the amount of coal it has), it exports more of this natural resource than any other country. Australian coal accounts for 29 percent of global coal exports.

APEC

Most of Australia's trade is focused in the Asia Pacific Economic Cooperation (APEC) region. APEC is a regional trade agreement that encourages more trade between the 21 countries in the area known as the Pacific Rim. These include the United States, Canada, Japan, South Korea, Australia, New Zealand, China, and Taiwan. APEC is Australia's largest regional trading partner.

Tourism

Tourism is one of Australia's top industries, with around 5.6 million tourists every year. The most popular tourist destinations are Sydney, Melbourne, and tropical parts of far northern Queensland. Australia's economy is dependent on tourism, and almost one in every 20 Australians is employed in the tourism industry. Tourists visit Australia from all over the world. New Zealand, the UK, Japan, the U.S., China, Korea, Singapore, Germany, and Malaysia are the top countries where people visit from. As China's economy is growing, the numbers of Chinese vacationers to Australia are increasing, too.

A Global Education

More and more students are choosing to study in countries other than their own, and education is a growing industry in Australia. Many international students choose to study in Australia every year. Around 370,000 students from 190 countries come to study in Australia annually. Australia not only helps educate students within Australia, but colleges and universities also set up branches in other countries. At any given time, around 120,000 students are enrolled in these offshore courses.

▼ *Tourists enjoy a beach in Queensland's Gold Coast, one of the most popular destinations for overseas visitors to Australia.*

GOING GLOBAL

Australia exports goods and services to around 200 countries around the world. However, the Asia-Pacific region accounts for the majority of Australian trade. Australia's largest export markets are Japan, China, the United States, the Republic of Korea, and New Zealand.

Government and Politics

Australia is a federation of states like the U.S. and Canada. The country has a democratic system of government, carried out by the federal parliament. The federal parliament is very similar to the British system, and is a gathering of the representatives elected by Australian citizens.

Compulsory Voting

All Australians age 18 and over have the right to vote, and, in fact, all Australians must vote or face a penalty. Australia is one of only 19 countries in the world—and the only English-speaking country—to enforce compulsory voting. The federal government must hold an election within three years of taking office.

Australia's Government

The Australian parliament, in the capital Canberra, is based on the British system. The parliament has two chambers: the House of Representatives and the Senate. The prime minister and other ministers are usually selected from the House of Representatives. Australia is divided into 148 federal electorates, and voters from each electorate must all choose one member of parliament (MP) to represent them.

▶ *Australia's parliament house is in the capital Canberra. When built in 1988, it was the most expensive building in the southern hemisphere.*

God Save the Queen!

Because Australia was once a British colony, the Queen of Britain is still Australia's head of state. In fact, Queen Elizabeth II is the monarch of 16 countries, including Australia. Since the Queen is based overseas, she has a representative in Australia called the governor-general. The governor-general approves all new laws and gives permission for the prime minister to hold elections. Even though the monarch is the official head of state, the Queen does not have anything to do with the day-to-day running of the country. The most important job in the country is that of the Australian prime minister, the leader of the political party that has the most members in the House of Representatives.

25

▼ *Queen Elizabeth II greets children on a visit to Australia during the Commonwealth Games in 2006.*

IT'S A FACT!

Australia is home to the world's largest constituency (870,768 sq miles/ 2,255,278 sq km), in Kalgoorlie, Western Australia.

Friends in the Asia-Pacific Region

In the early part of the twentieth century, Australia was quite isolated from the rest of the world. Since World War II, it has tried to build up relations with its neighbors around the Asia-Pacific region. Increasingly, relations with China are becoming more important to the Australian economy. China is Australia's largest two-way trading partner, and Australia has a large number of Chinese immigrants. Even the Australian prime minister, Kevin Rudd, can speak Chinese fluently!

IT'S A FACT!

During World War I (1914–18), troops from Australia, New Zealand, and Britain tried to capture the Gallipoli Peninsula in Turkey. They fought for eight months. More than 33,000 ANZAC (Australia and New Zealand Army Corps) troops died. Gallipoli is remembered on April 25 every year on ANZAC day, an Australian public holiday.

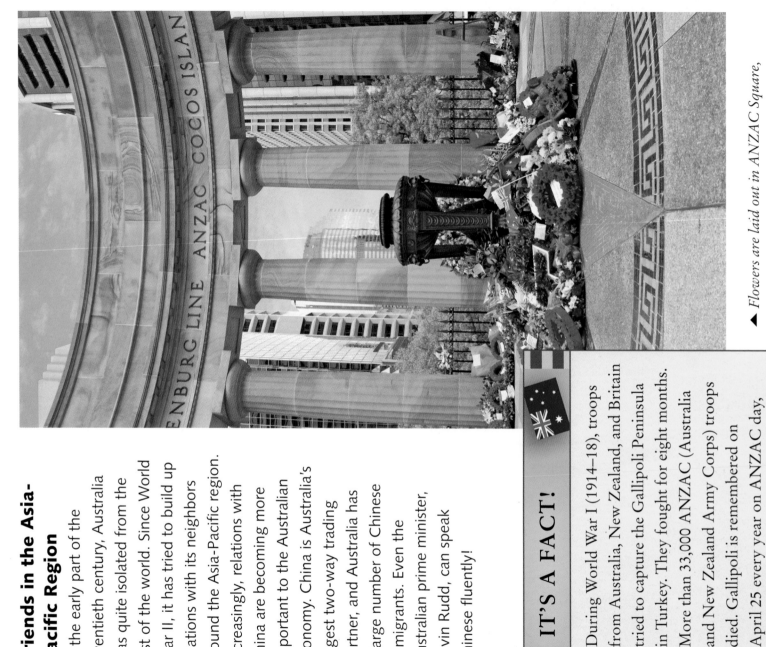

▲ Flowers are laid out in ANZAC Square, Brisbane, to commemorate the Australian soldiers who died in World War I.

Global Influence

Australia has long played a key role in international affairs. The country is heavily involved in organizations like the United Nations, the World Bank, the World Trade Organization (WTO), and the International Monetary Fund (IMF). Australia cooperates with organizations like the Association of Southeast Asian Nations (ASEAN) and the Asia Pacific Economic Cooperation (APEC). In 2007, Australia ratified the Kyoto Protocol, an international agreement to reduce greenhouse-gas emissions. This was a significant step, as Australia is one of the highest polluters per capita in the world.

International Relations

Because of its colonial history, Australia has strong ties with Britain. It is part of the Commonwealth of Nations, which includes Britain and other independent nations that were once British colonies. Australia also has strong ties to the U.S., which it supported in the wars in Korea, Vietnam, Iraq, and Afghanistan. The Australian army currently has around 3,000 troops overseas in countries including Iraq, Afghanistan, and Sudan.

▼ *Former prime minister John Howard talks to Australian troops in Baghdad, Iraq, in 2005.*

Australia in 2030

Australia is likely to experience some dramatic changes in the coming years, particularly in areas such as population, climate, and trade. The economy is expected to improve and, by 2030, Australia's GDP per person may have doubled, increasing the country's influence in the world.

Bigger Cities

In the future, it is likely that even more Australians will move from rural areas to the cities, and experts believe that over 90 percent of the population will be living in cities by 2030. As the cities were not originally designed for such large populations, the government will need to expand these areas. High-rise apartments will need to be built to house the growing population, and infrastructures such as train lines and bus routes will need to be extended to cater for more people.

▶ *Increasing numbers of young people are moving to cities such as Melbourne.*

A Larger, Older Population

Australia's population is set to grow to 25 million by 2030. Because life expectancy is increasing and fewer people are having babies, by 2030 a large proportion of Australia's population will have retired. In order to make sure there are still enough young workers to maintain the economy, Australia will need to increase immigration.

Dry Times Ahead

The overall temperature in Australia is set to rise by 0.36–3.6°F (0.2–2.0°C) by 2030 due to climate change. This will mean between 10 and 50 percent more days over 95°F (35°C). This will be a problem for Australia, as it already has the highest skin cancer rate in the world due to exposure to the sun's rays. By 2030, rainfall is expected to drop in most parts of the country. There will be more dry days, but when storms do come, they are likely to be stronger than in the past. Tropical cyclones will become more intense and sea levels will continue to rise.

▶ *Droughts are likely to become more frequent in the future due to climate change, and evaporation rates will increase.*

IT'S A FACT!

Environmental factors are likely to have a dramatic impact on Australia's farming industry in the coming years. Less rain, drier rivers, and more droughts could lead to a drop in agricultural production of up to 10 percent by 2030.

Glossary

Aboriginal a native or indigenous Australian.

barracks a group of buildings used by military personnel as housing or lodgings.

climate change the change in the Earth's weather patterns, especially those produced by global warming.

colony a territory under the immediate political control of a country.

continent one of the Earth's seven great land masses—Africa, Antarctica, Asia, Australia, Europe, North America, and South America.

democracy a form of government in which people vote for the leaders they wish to represent them.

displaced person someone who has been forced to move to a different place within their home country because of war or unrest.

drought a water shortage caused by a long spell with little or no rain.

economy the financial system of a country or region, including how much money is made from the production and sale of goods and services.

emissions substances that are emitted or released, such as gases from vehicle exhausts.

export to transport products or materials abroad for sale or trade.

federation a grouping together of smaller regions to create a larger political union.

greenhouse gas a gas such as carbon dioxide that traps heat in the Earth's atmosphere, produced largely from burning fossil fuels.

immigrant a person who has moved to another country to live.

indigenous native to a land or region.

opal Australia's national gemstone; nearly 90 percent of all the opals in the world come from Australia.

Pacific Rim the countries and cities located on the edge of the Pacific Ocean.

ratified the act of giving official approval to a formal document, such as a treaty or constitution.

refugee someone who has had to flee from their own country because of war or persecution.

resources things that are available to use, often to help develop a country's industry and economy. Resources could be minerals, workers (labor), or water.

soap opera an ongoing fictional series, usually broadcast on television or radio.

tabbouleh a Lebanese salad of bulgur (cracked) wheat, mint, tomatoes, onions, and parsley.

Further Information

Books

Australia
Earth's Continents
by Mary Lindeen
(Child's World, 2010)

Australia and Oceania
A True Book
by Mel Friedman
(Children's Press, 2009)

This is Australia
This is . . .
by Miroslav Sasek
(Universe Pub., 2009)

Focus on Australia
World in Focus
by Otto James
(World Almanac Library, 2007)

Living in the Australian Outback
World Cultures
by Jane Bingham
(Raintree Publishers, 2008)

Spotlight on Australia
Spotlight on my Country
by Bobbie Kalman
(Crabtree Pub., 2008)

Web Sites

http://www.australia.com
Australia's official tourism web site.

http://www.dfat.gov.au
The Australian government's Department of Foreign
Affairs and Trade web site.

http://www.multiculturalaustralia.edu.au
A site with lots of resources about multiculturalism
in Australia.

http://www.dreamtime.net.au
A site dedicated to Indigenous Australia.

http://www.acn.net.au
The Australian government's culture web site.

http://www.australia.gov.au
Gateway to many other sites on Australia.

Every effort has been made by the publisher to ensure
that these web sites contain no inappropriate or offensive
material. However, because of the nature of the Internet,
it is impossible to guarantee that the contents of these sites
will not be altered. We strongly advise that Internet access
is supervised by a responsible adult.

Index

Numbers in **bold** indicate pictures